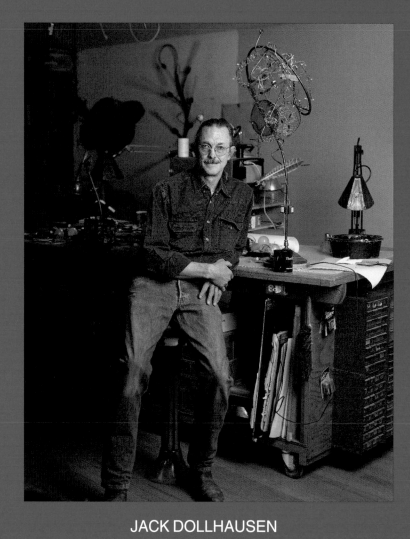

JACK DOLLHAUSEN

Jack Dollhausen: A 30 Year Start

Exhibition organized by Boise Art Museum in partnership with Salt Lake Art Center

Co-curated by Sandy Harthorn, Boise Art Museum and Ric Collier, Salt Lake Art Center

Essay by Aden Ross

EXHIBITION ITINERARY

BOISE ART MUSEUM
Boise, Idaho
December 14, 2001 - February 17, 2002

TACOMA ART MUSEUM
Tacoma, Washington
April 19, 2002 - June 16, 2002

SALT LAKE ART CENTER
Salt Lake City, Utah
October 19, 2002 - January 19, 2003

NORTHWEST MUSEUM OF ARTS & CULTURE
Spokane, Washington
March 20, 2003 - June 22, 2003

HOLTER MUSEUM OF ART
Helena, Montana
August 27, 2003 - October 26, 2003

The exhibition and publication have been made possible in part by the Beaux Arts Société, The Allen Foundation for the Arts, The Hackborn Foundation and the Andy Warhol Foundation for the Visual Arts.

Partial operating support is provided to the Boise Art Museum by its members, the Beaux Arts Société, BAM Exhibition Guild, JAMM, Collectors Forum, the City of Boise, the Idaho Commission on the Arts, and the National Endowment for the Arts.

Library of Congress
Cataloging-in-Publication Data

Jack Dollhausen, a 30 year start : exhibition organized by the Boise Art Museum in partnership with Salt Lake Art Center / exhibition co-curated by Sandy Harthorn, Boise Art Museum and Ric Collier, Salt Lake Art Center; essay by Aden Ross.
   p. cm.
"Boise Art Museum, December 14, 2001-February 17, 2002; Tacoma Art Museum, April 19-June 16, 2002; Salt Lake Art Center, October 19, 2002-January 19, 2003; Northwest Museum of Arts & Culture, March 20-June 22, 2003; Holter Museum of Art, August 27-October 26, 2003."
Includes bibliographical references.
  1. Dollhausen, Jack, 1941--Exhibitions. 2. Kinetic sculpture--United States--Exhibitions. 3. Light in art--Exhibitions. 4. Sound in art--Exhibitions. 5. Machinery in art--Exhibitions. I. Title: Jack Dollhausen. II. Title: Jack Dollhausen, a thirty year start. III. Collier, Ric, 1947- IV. Harthorn, Sandy, 1945- V. Ross, Aden Kathryn, 1944- VI. Boise Art Museum. VII. Salt Lake Art Center.
  NB237.D65 A4 2001
  730'.92--dc21
                                                                                                              2001006570

Cover: *Too Close*, 1988, wood, electronic circuitry, 48 x 31 x 3", Courtesy of the artist. Inside front and back cover: *Too Close*, detail

Credits: Kathleen Bettis, Editor; Geoffrey Beard, Design; Josyln and Morris, Boise, Idaho, Printer; Paul Lee, Photographer

THE BOISE ART MUSEUM GRATEFULLY ACKNOWLEDGES
THE FOLLOWING EXHIBITION SPONSORS AND LENDERS

SPONSORS

Beaux Arts Société

The Allen Foundation for the Arts

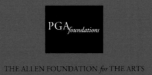

THE ALLEN FOUNDATION *for* THE ARTS

The Hackborn Foundation

The Salt Lake Art Center acknowledges the support of the
Andy Warhol Foundation for the Visual Arts
for making this collaborative project possible.

LENDERS

Ric Collier

Jack Dollhausen

Kenneth and Dorothy Holmes, Jr.

David S. and Deborah Lewy

Helga Redmann

Mr. and Mrs. Robert M. Sarkis

Beth Sellars

Boise Art Museum

Northwest Museum of Arts & Culture,
Spokane, Washington

Office of the President, Washington State University,
Pullman, Washington

FOREWORD

In 1978, the Boise Art Museum (BAM) organized a solo exhibition by artist Jack Dollhausen and, later that year, acquired one of Dollhausen's more humorous works titled *Minor Nation (Frog Pond)*. An interactive sculpture, *Minor Nation (Frog Pond),* when viewed from a distance resembles an abstract painting; yet upon closer inspection, revealed is a collection of colored wires, computer chips, lights and paint, a deconstruction of simple electronic technology that mimics more than magical amphibian sounds. Now, twenty-two years later, BAM, in collaboration with the Salt Lake Art Center, is honored to pay tribute to this artist by organizing and traveling a representative selection of Dollhausen's work in an exhibition aptly titled *Jack Dollhausen: A 30 Year Start.*

Acknowledged as one of today's foremost artists working in the Pacific Northwest, Jack Dollhausen was one of the early proponents of computerized art – a movement initiated in the 1960s in the Pacific Northwest. Dollhausen has dedicated a lifetime to creating what he refers to as "machines," computerized sculptural assemblages that react to the environment or the presence of a viewer through the utilization of motion, light and sound. In addition, Dollhausen has contributed to higher education for the past thirty-five years, as a professor of art at Washington State University, and has continued to exhibit his work internationally.

This second exhibition, co-curated by Sandy Harthorn, Curator of Art at BAM, and Ric Collier, Director of the Salt Lake Art Center, enables viewers to experience and to evaluate twenty-six important works created over the past thirty years. The exhibit is a testament to Dollhausen's work, his career, and his contributions to the arts.

Projects of this scope culminate from enormous allotments of time, energy and collaboration. I thank Jack Dollhausen for sharing his artistic vision, Sandy Harthorn for her determined engagement and vision, Ric Collier for enthusiastically supporting this partnership, and Aden Ross for her profound knowledge of Dollhausen's work and authorship of the catalogue essay. I owe a debt of gratitude to the many lenders to the exhibition and to BAM's entire professional staff for their dedication, support and spiritedness. On behalf of the Board of Trustees of the Boise Art Museum, I thank the Boise Art Museum's Beaux Art Société, The Allen Foundation for the Arts, The Hackborn Foundation and the Andy Warhol Foundation for the Visual Arts for providing the generous support required to bring this project to fruition. Finally, I thank BAM's partnering institutions, the Salt Lake Art Center, Tacoma Art Museum, Northwest Museum of Arts & Culture and the Holter Museum of Art for participating in the tour of this exhibition.

Timothy Close
Executive Director

INTRODUCTION

Jack Dollhausen is a curator's artist, a sculptor I have admired for many years and whose interactive sculptures garner praise from numerous museum professionals. Although Jack does not pursue the limelight, his computerized sculptures are represented in public and private collections across the country and in Europe. Once introduced to Jack's sculpture, art lovers and collectors are enchanted by his remarkable inventions, keen wit and juggling of art and sciences. To own a Jack Dollhausen sculpture is to live with a phenomenal machine whose quirks and idiosyncrasies take on personality and become part of your life and environment.

I imagine that Jack's mind is like an AT&T substation with miles and miles of wires carrying thousands of impulses, with ideas being conceived and transmitted at every turn of the way. He is a man who thinks on many levels, and just to follow along with him in a discussion is a mesmerizing experience. Jack's art encourages us to see the commonplace in a different light – to explore the what-ifs.

Figuratively speaking, the world has traveled light years since 1970 and so has Jack. The thirty years covered in the exhibition take us from early pieces such as *Midwest Summer Night's Dream (Bug Jar)*, based on the flickering light of fireflies, to newly created sculptures like *3PPB* which is a reflection on the dynamism of the nuclear age. Over the years, Jack has continued to address technical challenges and innovative expression in his work, all the while maintaining seemingly effortless spontaneity.

It is with great affection and pride that *Jack Dollhausen: A 30 Year Start* has been organized in concert with Ric Collier, Director of the Salt Lake Art Center. Ric's relationship with Jack spans both their careers and there is no bigger fan or friend to interpret and guide this exhibition. Ric's insight and knowledge of Jack's work has inspired us all. A particular note of appreciation is also extended to Aden Ross, who has so perceptively captured the spirit of Jack's work. Finally, we offer our deepest gratitude to Jack for his generosity in sharing his *living* machines and challenging us with incredible, thought-provoking sculpture.

Sandy Harthorn

Curator of Art

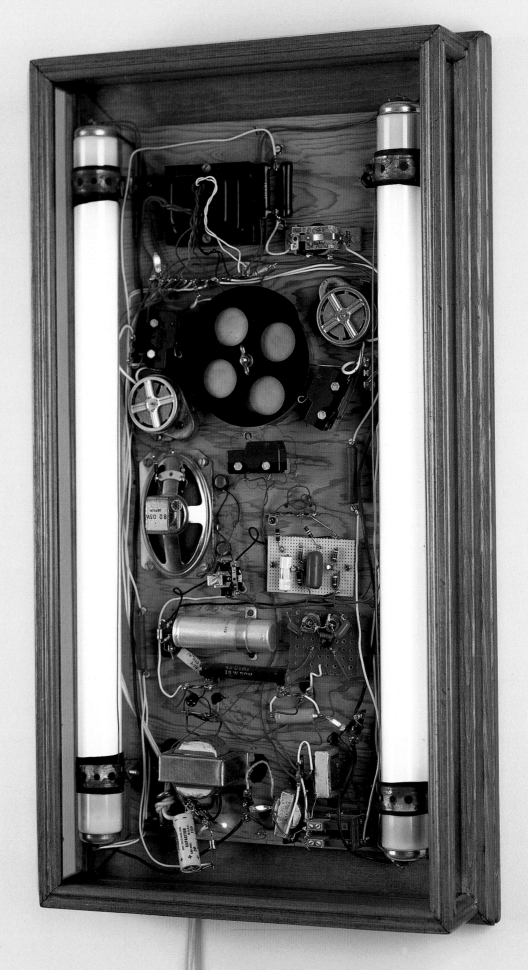

Prototype

PERSISTENCE OF VISION BY ADEN ROSS

Think binary numbers. Think the multi-layered fugues of Bach. Think a chopped and channeled hot rod, old flying saucer movies, a pond cloudy with algae, Las Vegas odds, and the coolest magic you know, and the hardest mathematics. Now put those thoughts into motion, and you get a feeling of Jack Dollhausen's art. I never believed, actually *believed,* in electrons until I encountered this work. Granted, we're engaged in mad tangos with sub-atomic particles every instant, but Jack makes the cosmic dance visible.

What are these pieces? Assemblages? Paintings in wire and light? They've been called "folk electronics," a description which Jack likes, although he associates that less with folk art than with folk science, as in medieval alchemy. Characteristically, Jack calls his work "machines," partly because he dislikes definitions in art, but mostly because they transform one kind of energy to another. If they are machines, as one of his collectors has said, they are "the most romantic machines" imaginable.

"All of my work comes from a pursuit of sound and light, movement and change, and unpredictable effects," Jack says. For thirty years, he has created light-space and sound-space, an invisible architecture surrounding each work; when a viewer breaks into that space, the piece responds in various ways. Thus, this art allows us to participate consciously in the perpetual, complex oscillations in the universe, an experience ranging from the merely startling to the downright psychedelic. In other words, here's your chance to flirt with radiant energy. And it flirts back.

folk electronics

When I first met Jack, I told him that his pieces make me think; he answered, "I would rather that they make you dance." Art and science, the intuitive and the rational, continually merge in his work. Typically, he once wondered what ionizing gas would look like if he could make it visible, rather like Einstein's considering what light would look like standing still. His mind works this way, always seeking to create visible beauty from invisible fact, the perfect symbiosis of art and science. Thus, understanding the science behind his art is essential to a full appreciation of its extraordinary richness.

It isn't coincidence that Jack was educated first as an engineer, a field he still views as an "organic activity" and an "existential pleasure." Having graduated with double degrees in math and fine art, Jack considers the binary number system one of his primary mediums, joking, "I paint with numbers." He also paints with semi-conductors, motion detectors, range-finders, infrared sensors, microphones, computer chips, and, most recently, Geiger counters. Every component must work; but it must also look right, which means hiding a great deal of the engineering. Thus, Jack toils at the guise of simplicity much as W. B. Yeats did in poetry: "A line will take us hours, maybe;/ Yet if it does not seem a moment's thought,/ Our stitching and unstitching has been naught."

Most of Jack's pieces, like shy little nervous systems, send out signals to search for signs of life in their vicinity. When they detect it, they whisper and flicker, growl, coo and flinch in synch with their viewer. Some are programmed to react differently each time in sequences which may not repeat in a human lifetime. Trying to please us with constantly new tricks requires billions (yes, *billions*) of permutations and combinations. If you're too loud or your movements are too large, they shut down. There are limits, after all, to friendship; and when familiarity becomes rudeness, they subtly introduce etiquette into aesthetics. The only way to stop them completely is to unplug them, an act akin to taking someone off life support.

Thus these are partially static *objets d'art* and partially dynamic improvisations to be performed with the viewer, an unexpected mix of art already created and art in the act of creation. Literally, this art needs you for it to be fully alive, and you need it: what a wonderfully understated and eloquent example of the mutual necessity of people and art.

Just as Jack's work redefines "interactive art," it also redefines "intelligent machines." When no one is present, some pieces work on their next reaction – think, nicker, burp. *Hummin' Stars* and *Grace* compose new

Having graduated with double degrees in math and fine art, Jack considers the binary number system one of his primary mediums, joking, "I paint with numbers."

You are too close!

music for their next visitors; *Grace* also concocts a new chime for every hour, as if it's bored with the

Westminster tradition. Both are smart enough never to repeat themselves, ever.

Smart is one thing, funny is usually another; but Jack's sense of humor also pervades his art. In one of his

earliest pieces, Jack anticipated the technology which now flashes words (such as the date and time) in mid-air.

When he had figured out how to create the effect with tiny lights on a swinging fishing pole, he characteristically

had it write the phrase, "Just to See It Work." In this exhibit, *Too Close* is programmed to sequence phonemes,

the sound fragments comprising language, in a pseudo-random fashion; but if a viewer comes too near, it

aligns its experimental syllables to blurt, "You are too close!" (Incidentally, when the piece was shown in

Germany, viewers heard it "speak" German.) Playfulness like this requires extremely unplayful computer logic

and calculations with threshold detectors.

Experiencing all this sensitivity, intelligence and humor, viewers almost sense Jack's living presence within

these pieces, an opportunity to engage with an artist's sensibility in a unique way.   Not only are you moving

within Jack's energy fields, you are virtually watching his brain work, seeing the minute, magical transformations

of neurons to ideas, of electrons to sound and light.

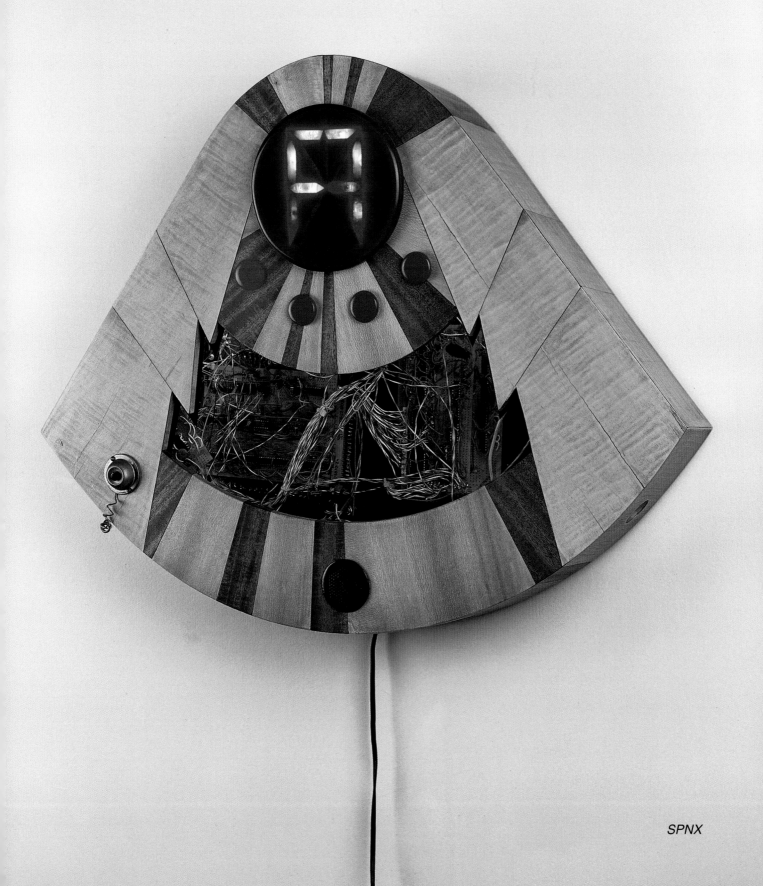

SPNX

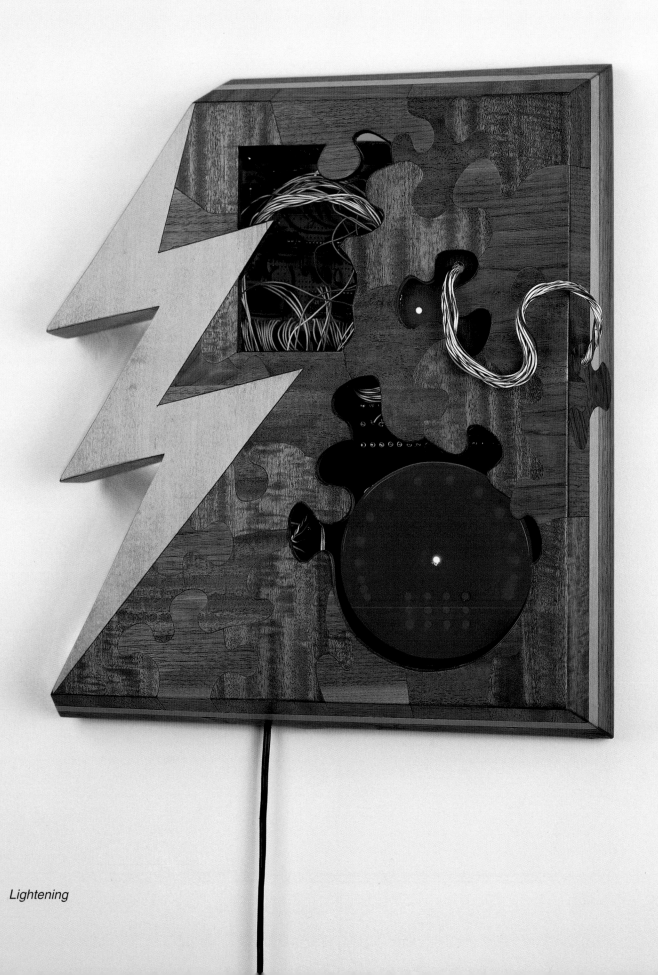

Lightening

Who is the magician behind these effects? Jack moves through the world much like his art: very conscious of his environment, intensely sensitive to people, always making connections, and presenting a deceptively simple surface.

He lives in a compound half hidden on a hilltop in downtown Pullman, Washington, which a friend named "Dogpatch" – gone to bedrock, gone to seed, gone to the critters and the spiders – a bit like the semi-vacant lot where you played as a child. His studio, which he calls his shop, he designed and built from the ground up, reminiscent of an old-fashioned car repair garage, but with an oak gymnasium floor characteristically recycled from the university nearby. Inside are boxes of transistors and diodes, dead oscilloscopes, overflowing plants, old computer monitors, coils of wire, soldering guns and Geiger counter tubes and sonar detectors and who knows whatall, everywhere. You get the sense that someone *lives* here, and very intensely. Unfinished pieces literally hang around – one, shaped like a brain in baling wire, is suspended from the ceiling; another unravels a tapestry of mysterious sensors and silicon chips; everywhere wires poke out like tentacles waiting to come to life. If not partially "blinded," finished pieces detect each other, flashing and snarling in electronic dogfights. Anything could come out of this place: a synthesized opera, a drag racer, an underground radio station broadcast, a bomb.

The artist, like the place, hides behind a deceptive surface, defying you to categorize him. Restless, he moves with lanky grace, talks with an off-beat lyricism; underneath hums something subtle and faintly dangerous, like radioactivity or irony. But Jack's persona of the folksy inventor hand-rolling his cigarettes lasts for about three sentences. Soon you're traversing every topic from the geologic history of eastern Washington to Fourier analysis of Bach.

On one level, of course, Jack is the archetypal inventor jerry-rigging the most unlikely materials into art. First and foremost, he insists that his art is about "stuff," physical things, an extension of how he tackles life in a sensuous and tactile way. He says, "Art is moving materials around. It is an activity which ends up with *things*, not representations of an idea." More important, moving things around is his way of thinking, not preparing to think.

Jack loves working with his hands and feels slightly wistful that the newest technology keeps his hands more on a computer keyboard than muscling sheet metal or shaping clay. Even before Marshall McLuhan popularized the idea, Jack felt that "the medium *is* the message." Materials are an extension of the self, just as the car is an extension of the body, or the computer is an extension of the brain, or the studio is an extension of the artist.

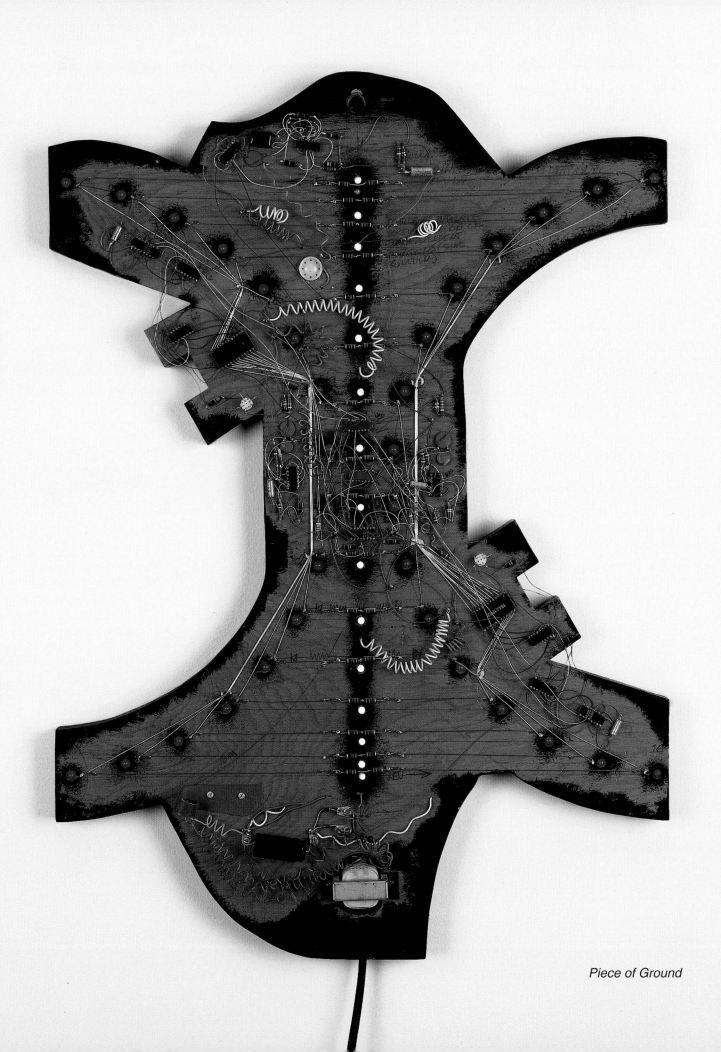

Piece of Ground

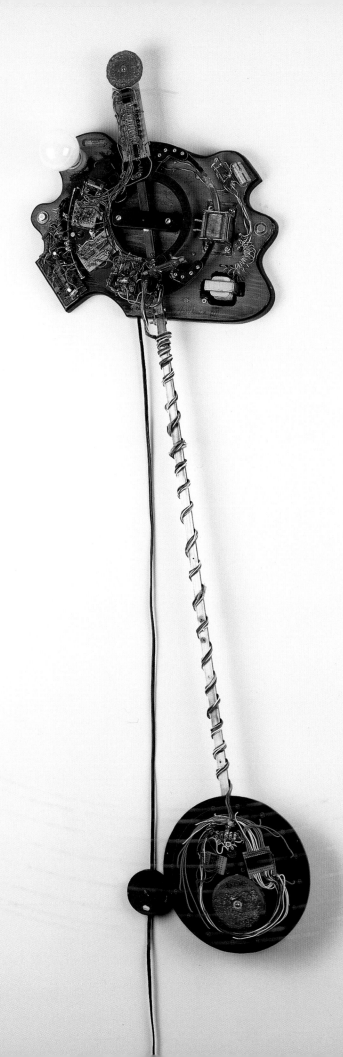

Transient Perpetuity

At first, Jack mostly used recycled parts and found objects, and he still watches out for things he can adapt and re-use (most recently the flash units from a hundred outdated disposable cameras). His new materials come from unlikely places like the Grange in downtown Pullman, which he terms his "art store." To people who consider his materials "cold," he has a droll response: "Maybe we're reluctant to leave a warm, wet, carbon-based life for a silicon-based one."

Jack's love of materials strongly affects the containers for his work. As a former builder of guitars, he is a meticulous craftsman, in love with beautiful woodworking. While the lethal voltages in early pieces like *Prototype* required simply being covered, his early containers also recall Joseph Cornell's mysterious and delicate boxes.

However, even in pieces with the most elegant cabinets, like *SPNX* and *Lightening*, the insides keep creeping out, the wiring naturally following the angles and curves of their containers. These "spills" illustrate one of many contradictions inherent in Jack's work – in this case, the ongoing tension between the "inside" and the "outside." We seem to be looking inside a machine or behind a stage set, which teases us into assuming that we have somehow traced the source of their illusions.

Later, Jack felt that the use of wood or leather added a complication, "a preciousness that was too blatantly meaningful." Besides, he said, "If I'm going to create life, I'll create it from scratch, not with something that was once alive." Although Jack now de-emphasizes containers *per se*, his aesthetic still demands close attention to other formal considerations like the overall shape, the frame, or the background "painting" of each piece. He has always liked the final look of an unidentifiable object found in the dusty corner of an old blacksmith's shop, typical of the innate modesty of this man and his work.

Jack's love of materials also provides one key to his creative process. For example, as a graduate student, he wondered what he could do with all those pinball machines he had bought; thus began his lifelong affair with electricity and flashing lights. Long ago, he found ten old Geiger counter tubes and years later decided to make pictures out of radiation. If he creates wiring diagrams at all, he draws them *after* a piece is built, in case it needs repair. As the poet E. E. Cummings said, "Since feeling is first," the "syntax of things" should come later.

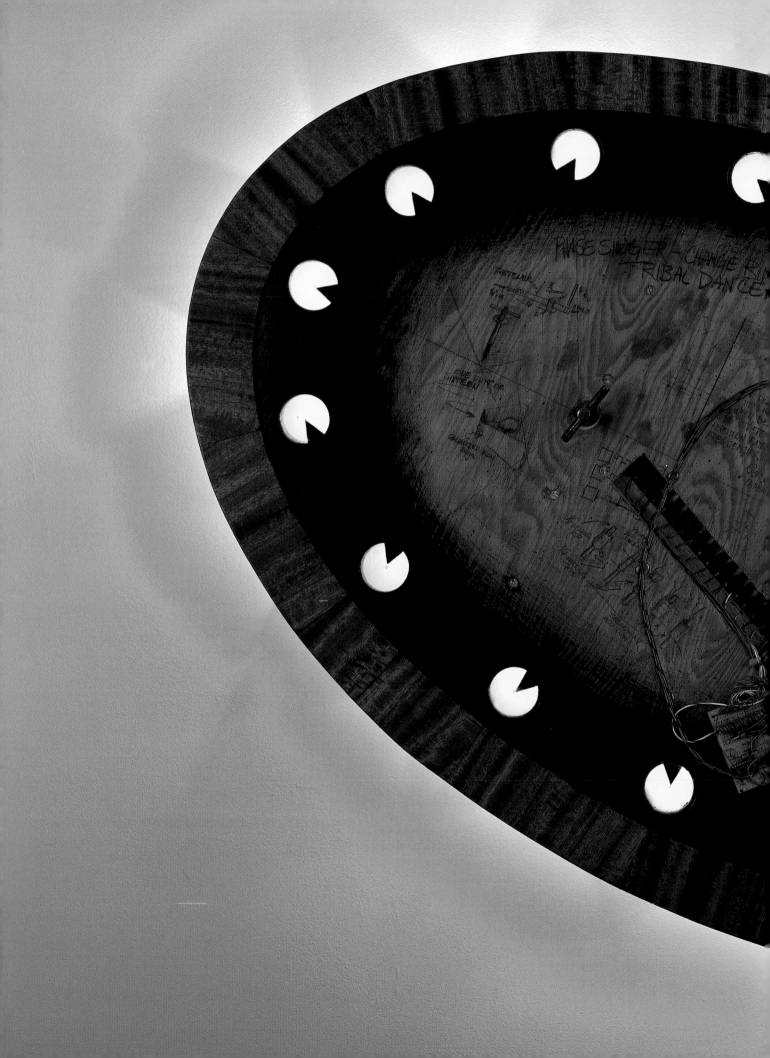

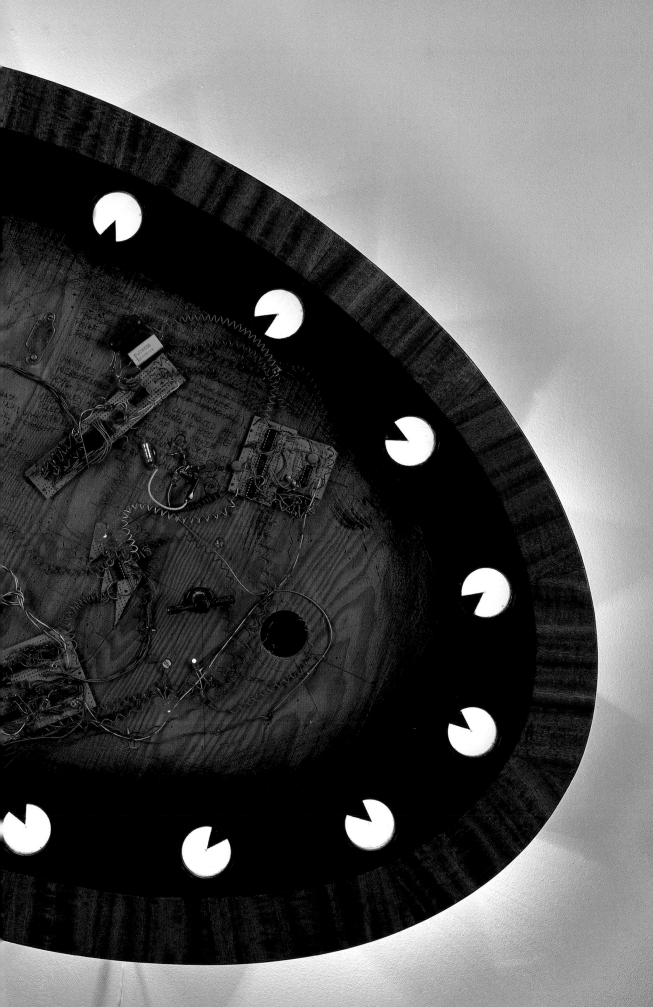

Dancer

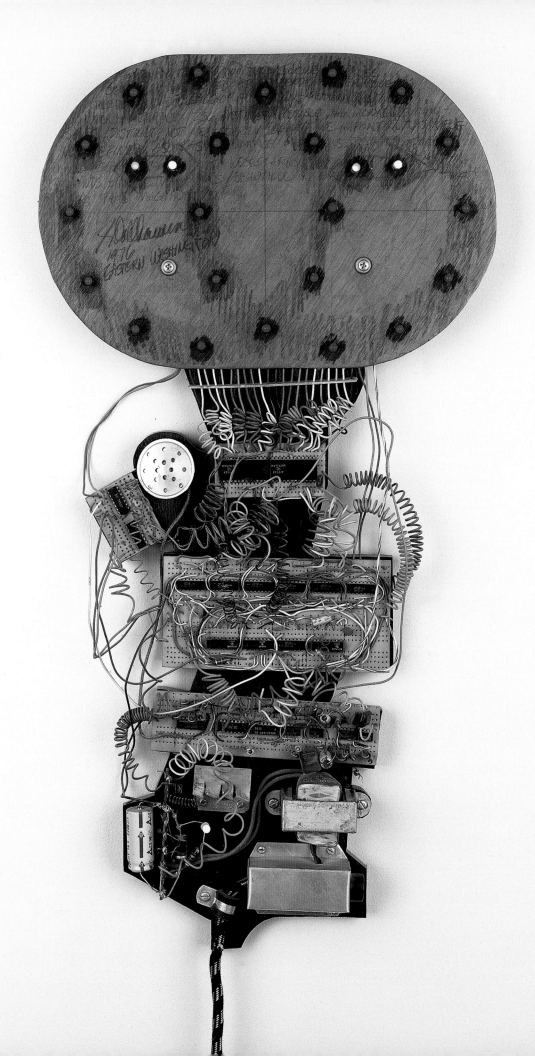

Esu

While Jack builds his machines, he doesn't think of images, but usually allows the circuitry itself to determine the shape of the piece. *Maxine*, for example, was named after a dog who helped him arrange the grid of lamps during construction. Each piece contains a "navel," central motion or sound detectors, in front of which Jack stands to decide which variables he wants to manipulate to make the piece relatively calm or excitable.

Then comes his favorite part of the process: playing with subtle adjustments in speed, brightness and sound, listening to it while he works on it. At some point, he says, his relationship to the piece takes over from the physical building, and he begins to sense its own identity. After that, it may take months to choreograph it, to match its form and personality. A piece is finished when he is "satisfied that it is a *thing*, something that can stand alone."

If the medium is the message, then the technology of the past logically becomes the art of the present. Obviously, Jack has an intimate, if constantly changing, relationship to technology. Long before today's novelty lamps, he experimented with lights which would illumine with a clap or a whistle, but his methods were so imprecise that the bulbs also reacted mysteriously to changes in temperature. A woman who bought one enthused, "Hell, it's got soul." When Jack related the story to a scientist, he responded with, "Hell, it's poorly designed and doesn't work worth a damn." Delighted but thoughtful, Jack adopted the scientist's name for the pieces – "Zingers" – and began to focus even more on the element of chance in his work.

Jack's design remains more digressive than ever, intentionally seeking the unexpected. The Zinger story illustrates how he has partially discovered and partially invented the engineering he needed to create unanticipated effects. Twenty-five years ago, using a primitive hand-held keyboard, he built his own computer, replete with his own original operating system. Since it had no storage capacity, he also invented a method for keeping information on cassettes, an illustration of how this artist's amazing intelligence and creativity extend into every aspect of his work.

From that point forward, Jack has been racing with developing technology. Now, of course, all his circuits are silicon chips which are so small that only robots can manipulate them. While they are far more reliable and straightforward, they are less material and take the poetry out of his hands. His older pieces, with all their soldered wires and bulky intersections, contain "an innocence and pain" that he doesn't feel when he types computer code to fourteen uncommitted pins on a computer chip. Still, he grins, he always tries to "regain his virginity" with pristine technology.

Fortunately, the newest technology can create very magical effects, nearly hiding the physical chips and allowing Jack to make the invisible ever more visible. It requires a thirty-year perspective to appreciate the technological developments in Jack's art. *Prototype* (1968) uses mostly electrical motors and relays, and it signals the transition between mechanical and electronic elements in Jack's work. *Esu* (1976) incorporates Jack's earliest use of LED's (light-emitting diodes, those barred lights appearing on digital watches). Significantly, the title refers to the African demon who engages in annoying but not dangerous activities, such as breaking your shoelaces. However he can, Jack celebrates the irrational world by disrupting the rational functioning of electronic circuitry.

Like so many of his later pieces, *Midwest Summer Night's Dream (Bug Jar)* (1977) is far more complex than it appears, running a "pseudo-random hardware iteration;" in other words, it was Jack's first full-fledged attempt to make a machine unpredictable, like the flight of a trapped bug. Successors to "*Bug Jar*" are *Chance of Laws* (1977) and *Solve/Dissolve* (1990), which ran ever more complicated programs for generating pseudo-random behavior.

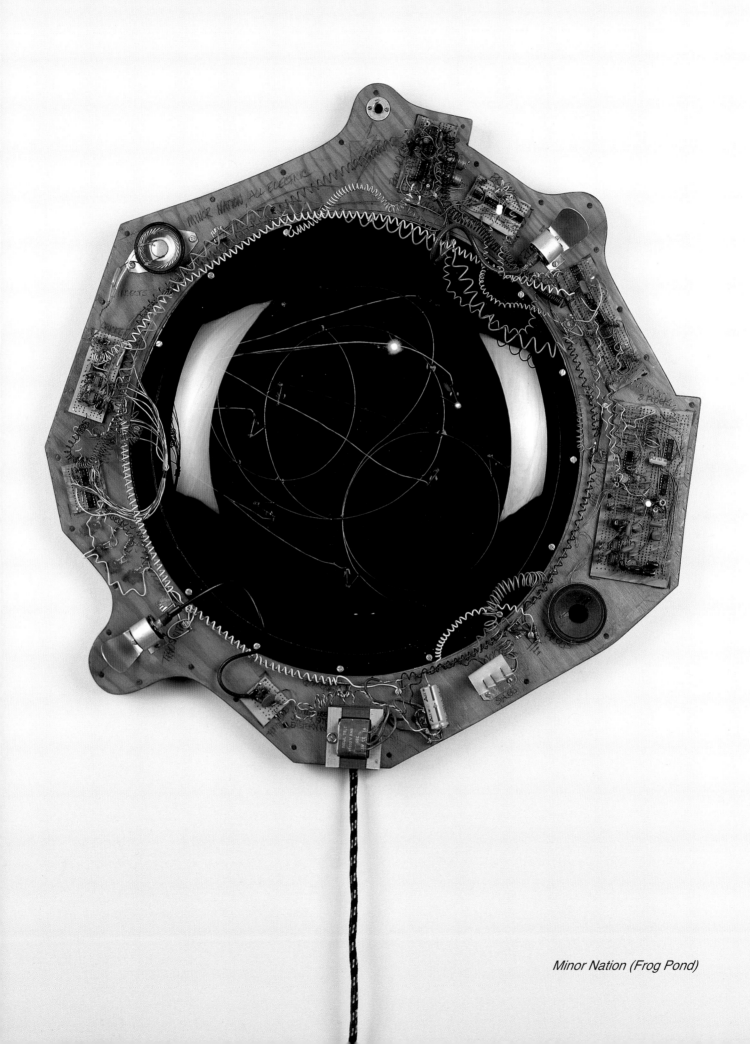

Minor Nation (Frog Pond)

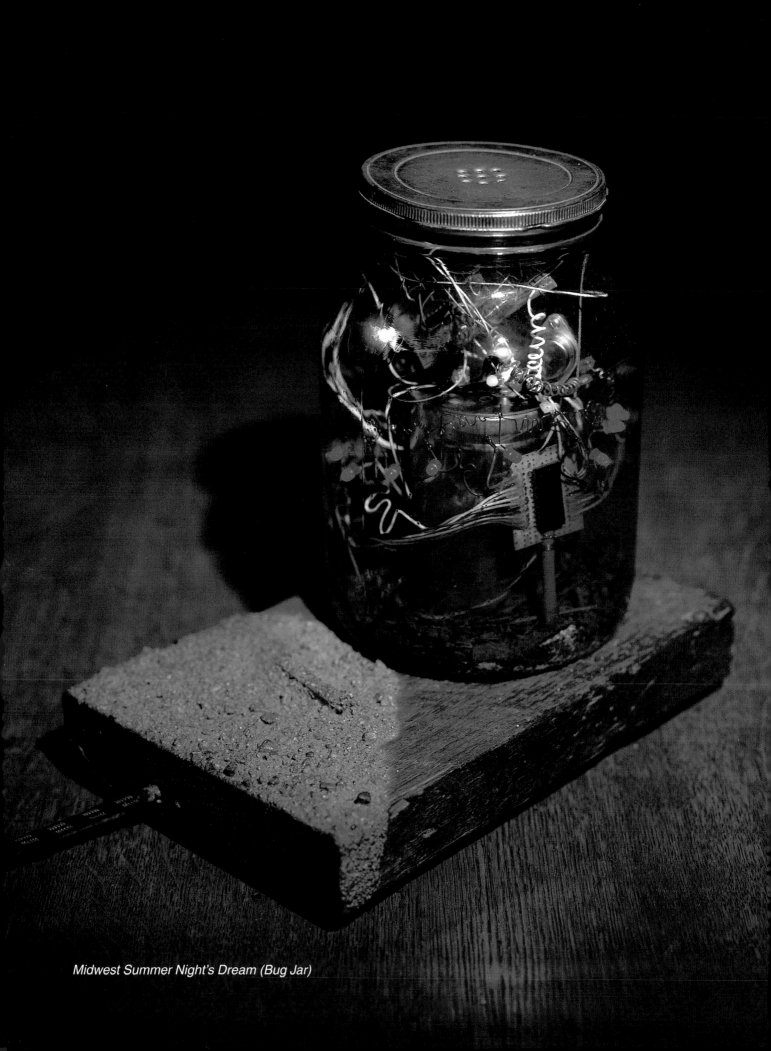

Midwest Summer Night's Dream (Bug Jar)

Jack's first embedded computer is in *A Walk Around the Pond* (1982), while *Hummin' Stars* (1989) is Jack's first piece to make music. And finally, in *Miner's Canary* (1986-7), he first used a Geiger counter to make visible the radiation constantly bombarding us. By coincidence, this piece was shown in Europe during the Chernobyl disaster, which triggered displays as enlightening as they were terrifying.

Regardless of Jack's technical landmarks, he continues to transform inelegant scientific fact into spectacular sensory experience. If these pieces did nothing, if they refused to perform and merely sulked on any given day, they would still be beautiful dancers sitting on a bench, in costumes rare and delicate, creatures who couldn't choose not to be exotic, even in the dark. They are never "off."

They merely rest. They seem to sleep, but actually they wait. And some plan.

conversation pieces

To Jack, art is not theoretical; it needs to be experienced rather than interpreted. Nonetheless, his art is as intellectually stimulating as it is aesthetically provocative, rewarding contemplation almost as much as the experience of it. Even Jack admits that artists make "conversation pieces;" however, by that he means that he is most interested in his viewers' feelings, intuitions or vague hunches that bring them back to the dialog.

One of the delightful contradictions in Jack's work is his shaping of the latest technology and inorganic materials like silicon and steel into organic forms suggestive of prehistoric creatures or imaginary flowers. Why these forms? He says that his greatest inspiration comes from nature.

He fell in love with the Palouse country where he lives while on a hitchhiking odyssey that took him to every state in the nation. Three decades later, he still relishes the area's microclimates and miniature ecosystems: for hours, he will stare into a pond and wait for minute changes, or study orb weaver spiders spinning webs, or examine how cells grow faster on one side of a plant stalk than on the other. "Nature doesn't make any moves that don't work," he says. "No kinks." When he returns to his studio, he tries not only to make things function the same way, but also to look like living things.

One of his most direct evocations of nature is *Minor Nation (Frog Pond)*, with layered insect and frog-like sounds which build to a chorus as someone approaches. He finished it one midsummer while a cricket sang outside. Jack said, "The experience was one of drawing from life." In a similar vein, *A Walk Around the Pond* creates scintillating patterns of varying brightness to mimic light reflected off the surface of moving water.

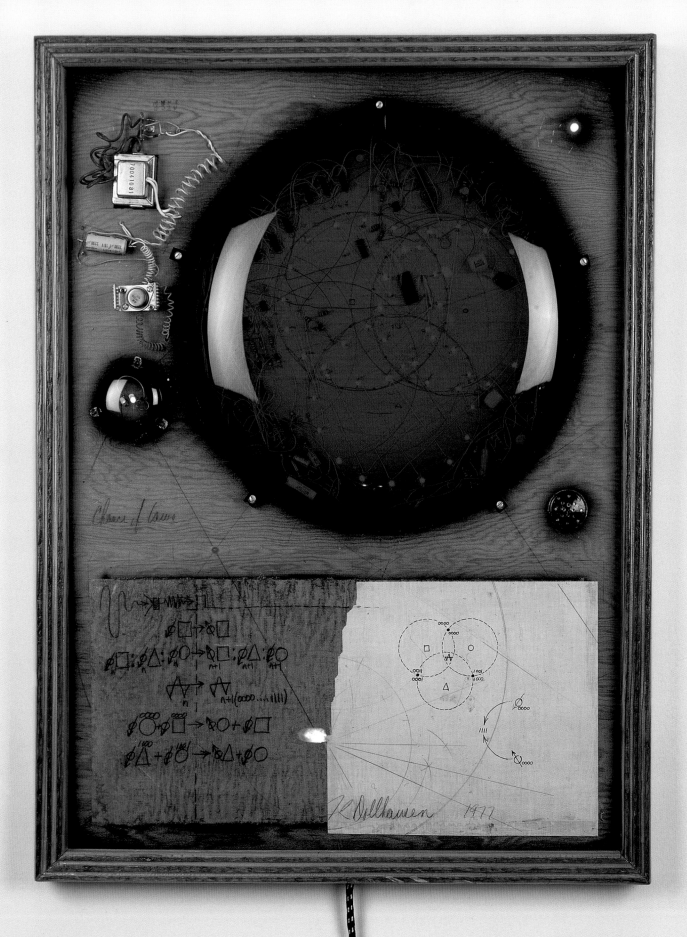

Chance of Laws

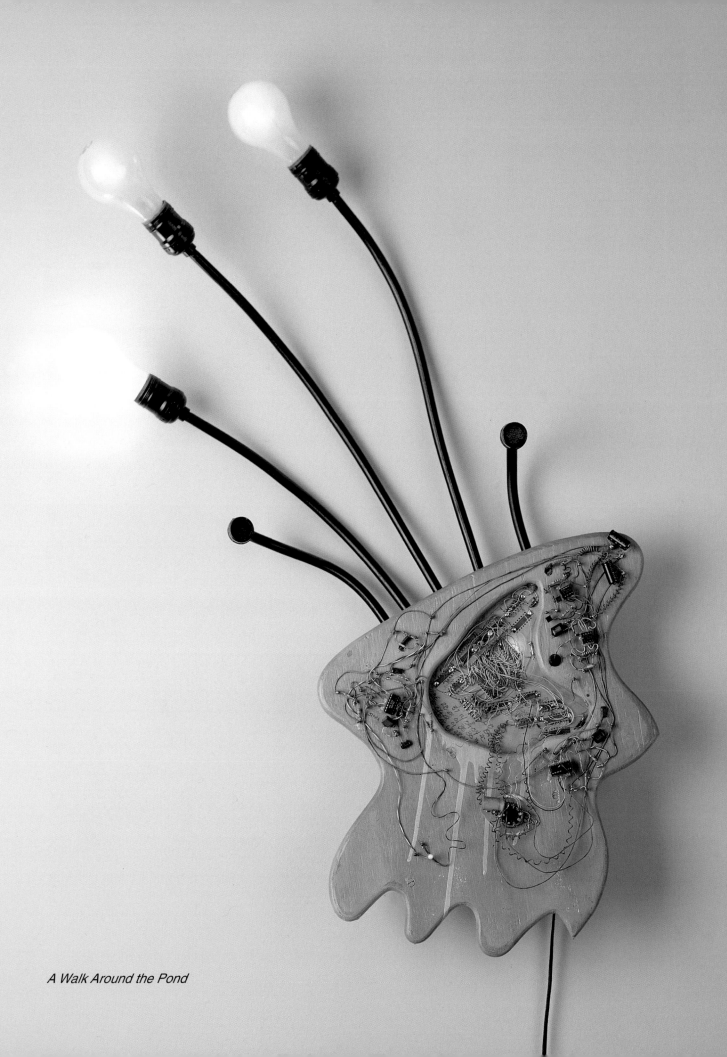

A Walk Around the Pond

To date, Jack has named five of his works *Dancer*, clearly a concept which intrigues him. Because so many of these pieces use detectors to see and respond to their viewers with light and sound, they tease us into increasingly flagrant physical movements – i.e., dancing with them. Laugh all you want – until you meet one. When approached, *Dancer 4*, for example, responds with surging lights and a whooshing sound, all changing pitch according to its own composition. Its invisible light-space and sound-space even contain a "sweet spot" of maximum response to minimal movement. Amazing in itself, but there's more: *Dancer 4* changes its own sweet spot over a few days; if its partner approaches too close, it becomes strident and unresponsive.

When I asked Jack what inspired his "Dancer" series, he quoted Yeats' poem "Among School Children": "O body swayed to music, O brightening glance,/ How can we know the dancer from the dance?" In his work, the viewer and the art, the dancer and the dance, are truly inseparable. More than that, Jack's dancers embody his attitude toward the world. While he doesn't formally dance – indeed, he said, "don't ask" – he is an incurable romantic and a fine singer, a man who dances with life, with his own art, and with us.

Light has more substance for Jack than for most people: he seems to capture it, juggle it from hand to hand, then flick it away like sparkling shooter marbles. "I am in love with light," Jack says, "because I can move it around without friction." His work doesn't merely use light; it is *about* light, like quantum physics or the paintings of Georges de La Tour, an artist whose use of light he admires more than Caravaggio's. Light as both form and content, of course, underlies many mythical and religious accounts of creation.

The "persistence of vision" is a term used for the optical phenomenon which occurs when the eye connects dots of light, whether you move your head quickly from side to side, blurring points of light to lines, or a mechanical device moves the light points for you to form lines or even words. Jack constantly depends upon this trick of our eyes to make us experience light in his art, almost to feel its touch. After dancing with his work, you can never again forget that you are constantly moving through this primary form of electromagnetic radiation in the universe, in both its visible and invisible manifestations.

"I am in love with light," Jack says, "because I can move it around without friction."

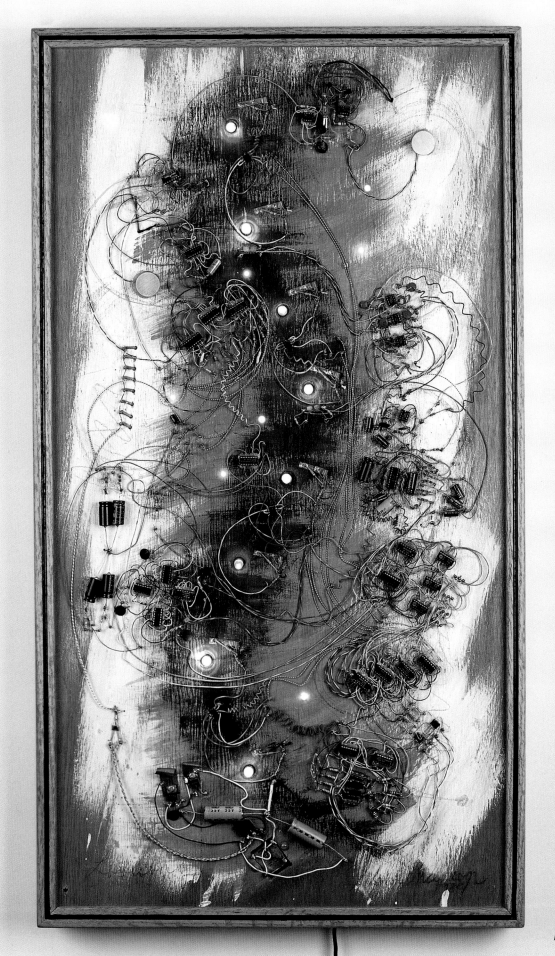

Lovesong

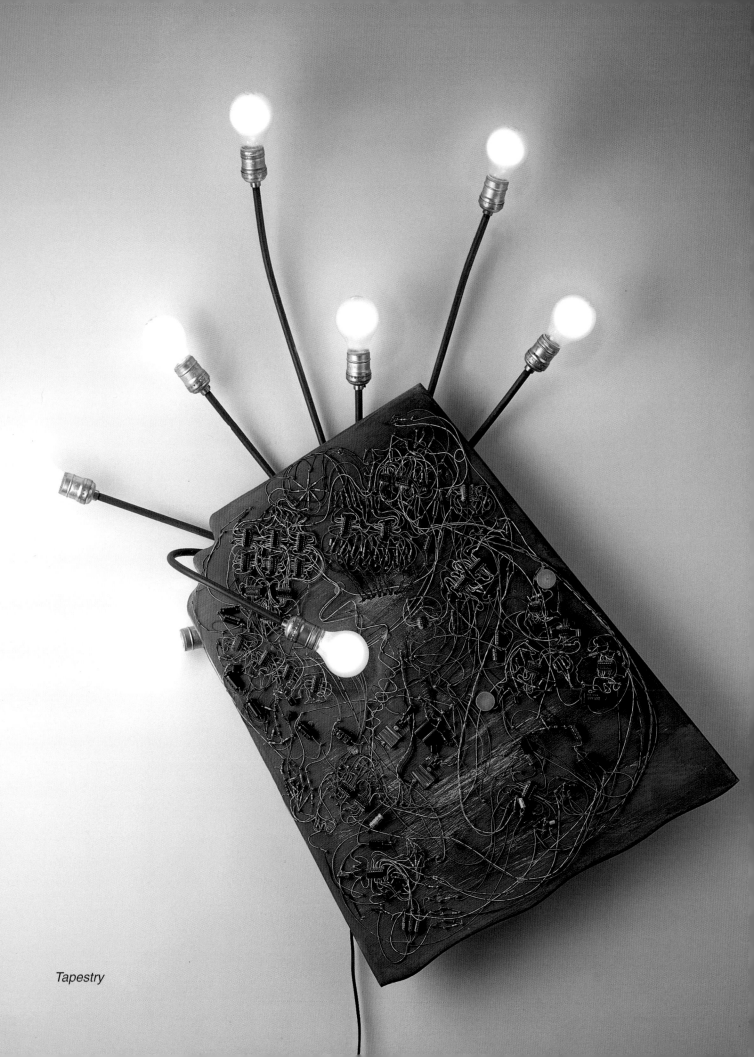

Tapestry

While Jack denies that his pieces play "music," he admits that he created some as musical instruments. He built and played guitars too long to consider an instrument merely a "circuit which resonates," and music does build on two of Jack's favorite mediums, time and mathematics. When the viewer plays Jack's instruments by moving around their architectural sound-space, some, like *Lovesong*, respond with soprano beeps and bass thrums, while others resonate in frequencies and tones which occidental cultures associate with music.

Since a single note from a piano or French horn contains many different individual frequencies (hence, Fourier analysis of Bach), imagine the complexity of creating the chorus of frogs in *Minor Nation (Frog Pond)* or the chords and harmonies of *Grace*. In fact, Jack recently re-worked *Grace* away from its speakers, separating the sound so he could hear and record it on a CD. He discovered that its music was much richer than he had thought, full of unexpected sounds and complex phrasing, much like the synthesized music of Karlheinz Stockhausen. The auditory opulence of *Grace* caused him to wonder, "How far ahead of me will my work go?" Marina Abramovic, a contemporary Balkan artist, feels the same way: "Learn from your own art because it is so much further along than you are."

Jack says his instruments produce "fake music," nonetheless allowing that they do "generate whole number frequency ratios and self-defined sequences of sounds." Perhaps Debussy's definition of music better fits Jack's work: "Music is the space between notes." Whether it's the notes themselves or the vibrant spaces between, it sounds like music to the rest of us.

fake music

Jack's art, like Anthony Powell's novel and the Poussin painting upon which it was based, "dances to the music of time." His pieces require far more time from their viewers than most art, partly because they perform in real time, differently each time, and often take years or lifetimes to repeat sequences. How does one build time into visual art? Jack uses pseudo-random computer programming, which minimally creates 26 x 26 x 26 x 26 (nearly half a million) different patterns.

Some of his pieces mark time directly, as unique and charming clocks. His public sculpture in Spokane, Washington, entitled *Time After Time*, is a huge clock without a read-out, but with a new chime for each hour. In this exhibit, *Transient Perpetuity* looks like a clock to communicate the sensation of time, while it actually adds time to the natural kinetics of a pendulum. To keep moving, its pendulum requires a periodic jolt from a tiny motor with a sensitive governor – in Jack's words, a "real bitch to build." In addition, the lights embedded on the pendulum play on our persistence of vision, embodying time on a small scale. While the pendulum gives it "perpetuity," the required stimulus makes it "transient." Consider how different the piece would be to depict "perpetual transience" instead.

Years ago, Jack wrote on his shop wall with a felt pen, "This is a competition with entropy." Since entropy is the tendency toward disorder in the universe, does that quotation imply that art *combats* disorder in a competition? Or that art competes *with* disorder, attempting to be more disordered than entropy itself?

For Jack, the latter is true. While some of us might associate art with order, Jack seeks the opposite, creating as much entropy as possible in his art. Characteristically contradictory, he uses the techniques of technology and engineering, which establish order through design, to undercut their premises in art. Naturally, some of his favorite images are of Jean Tinguely's technology going berserk and tearing itself apart.

To Jack, silence is order and noise is maximal information, so he first builds circuits to make as much noise as possible. Once he has created a disorderly system for his raw working material, he can introduce as much order as he wishes by filtering out unwanted effects. He puts it simply, "My art is a total acknowledgment of entropy."

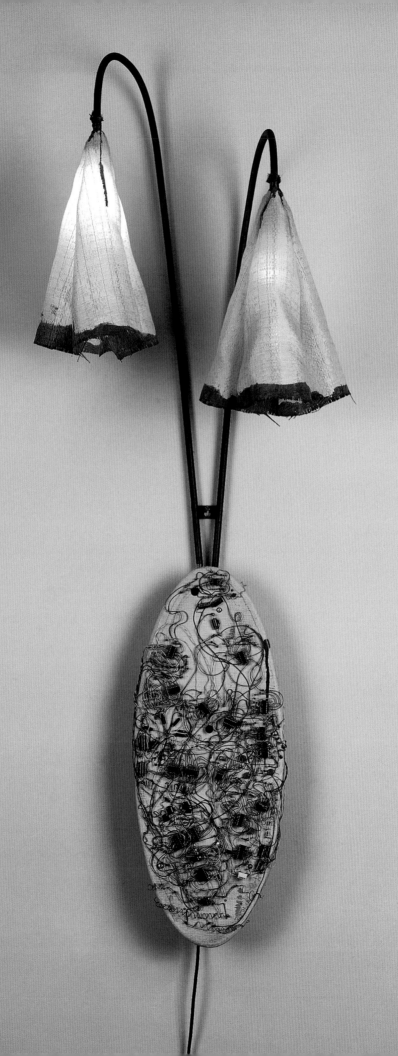

Pinup

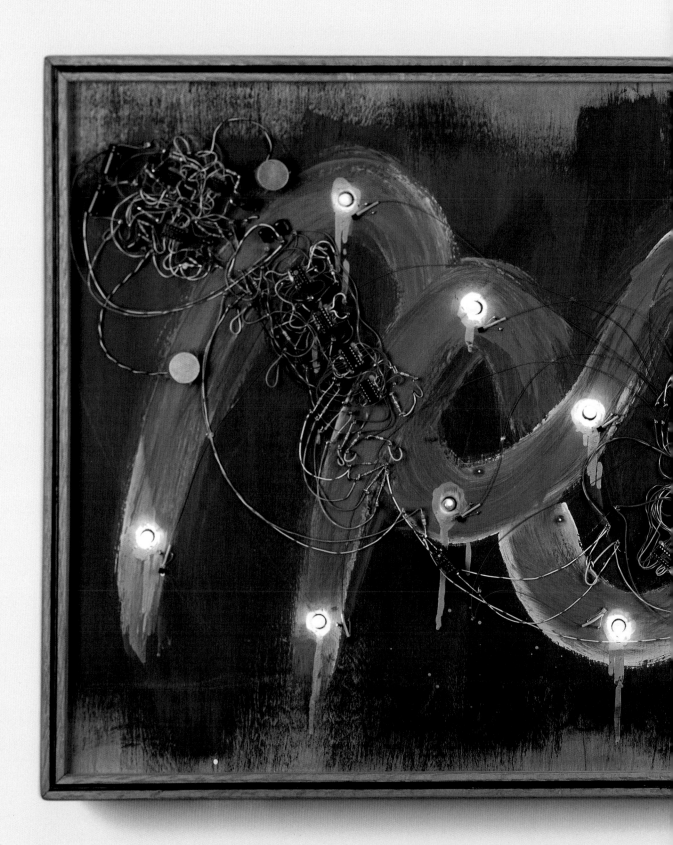

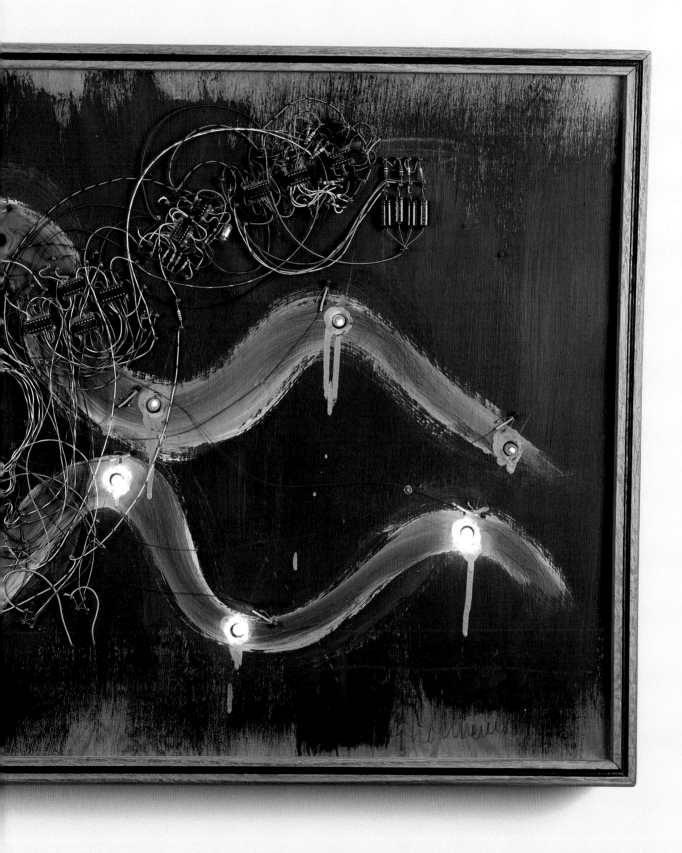

Waves

How does one build

time into visual art?

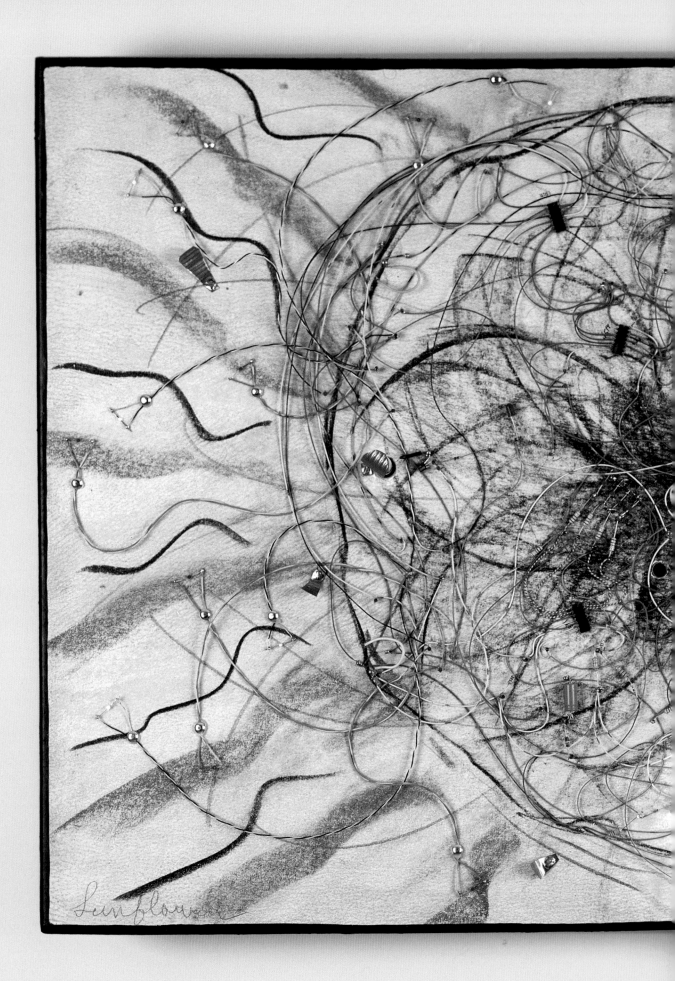

Sunflower

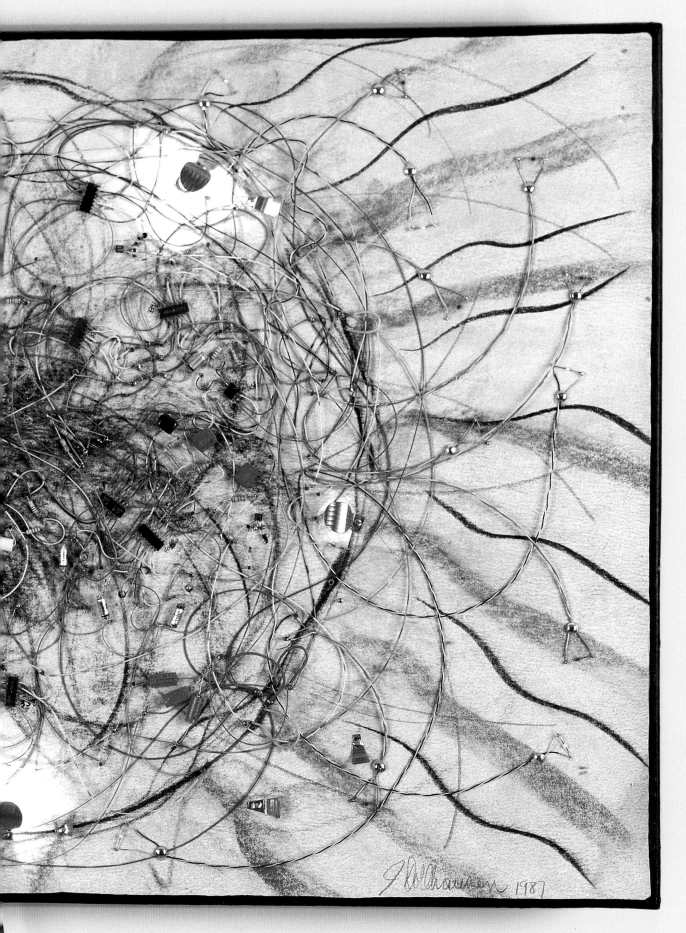

Sunflower

Jack's search for disorder in his art is ironically complicated by the innate predictability of devices designed to produce precise intervals. He bemoans the fact that true randomness isn't possible; after a quadrillion emissions, for example, the same information reappears. This may not bother the average person, but Jack is far from the average person.

In this respect, *Midwest Summer Night's Dream (Bug Jar)* presented one of his earliest challenges. He wanted a tiny light to "search" the perimeter of a jar in an unpredictable, arhythmic, back-and-forth motion like a bug. To accomplish that, he wired a circuit called a pseudo-random sequence generator, which ultimately produced, in his words, "delightfully weird results." Once he added audio pickup and circuitry to change the sequence's starting point, his "bugs" became more frantic as one tapped more loudly on their jar.

Over the years, he has vastly compounded the pseudo-randomness in his art. For example, he built *Solve/Disolve* mostly to run his algorithm for pseudo-randomness, generating on a grid both static patterns and rhythmic variations of lights. Possibly Jack's most cerebral work, it is "numbers made manifest;" visually it looks like a two-dimensional skull containing a square brain. Occasionally, Jack prints out his pseudo-random programming in graphs that look ever so much like brain scans or lie detector tests. Perhaps they are a little bit of both.

While chance itself seems to be the order of Jack's disorder, he is well aware that chance has its own laws, possibly harder to break than predictability. Two of his pieces are entitled *Chance of Laws*, not because they generate random sequences but to underscore this artist's private, ongoing battle with *any* law – scientific, aesthetic, technological, psychological, you name it.

In his first *Chance of Laws*, three interlocking circles of light respond to sound, but the lights repel each other when they meet at any intersection. Think about that. Intersections and meetings, attractions and repulsions, all predicated on chance. Perhaps Jack is less interested in the laws of chance than he is in asking what chance there might be for any laws to operate – on himself, on his work, on us. As unexpected as a jazz riff, an improvised dance step or a short circuit, Jack's questioning the chance of laws is a really subtle form of anarchy.

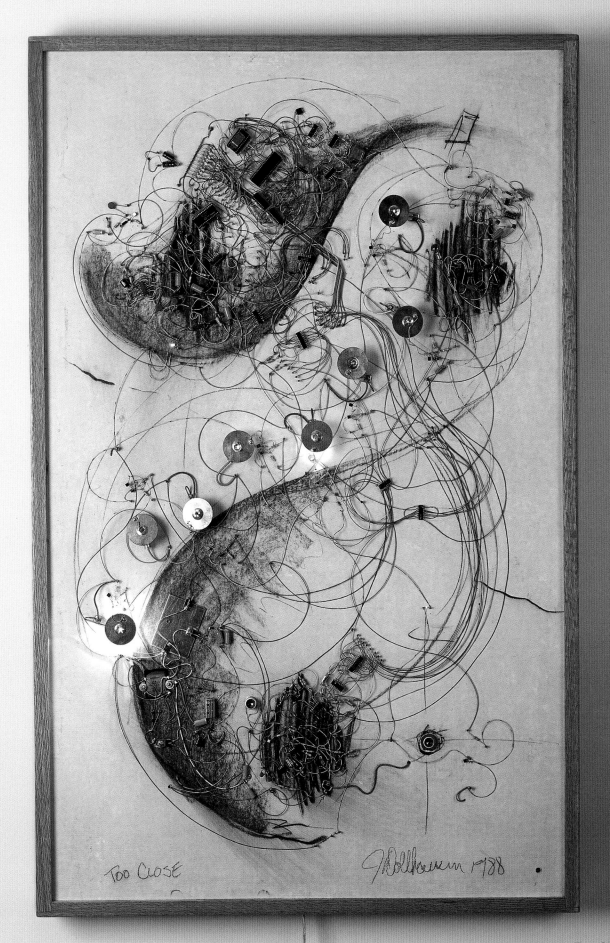

TOO CLOSE   Dollhausen 1988

Too Close

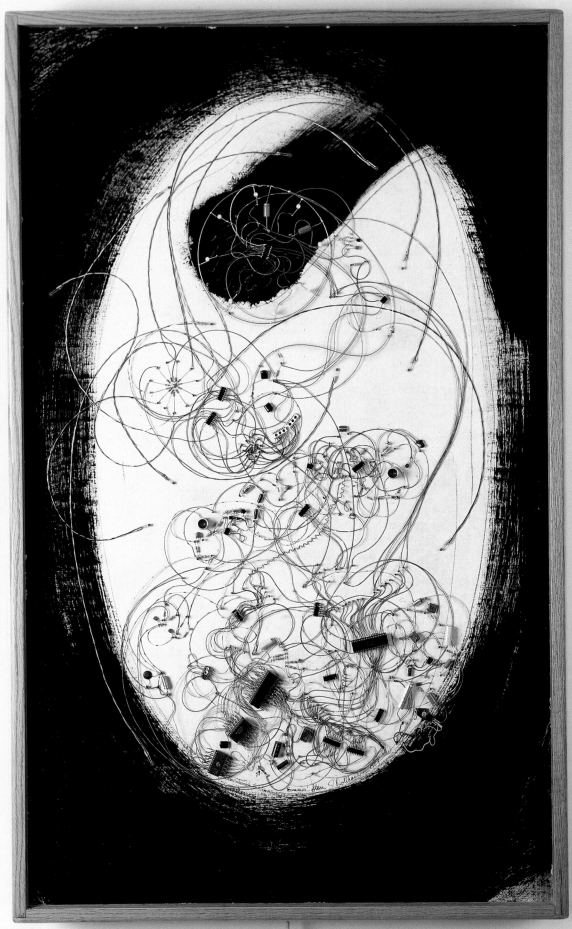

Hummin' Stars

creativity squared

Jack's artistic career has spanned everything from pinball machines to computers, has included ceramics, wood sculpture, blown glass, welded steel and cast bronze. That doesn't include the spinning mandalas, soundtracks of men pounding roofing nails, and simulated explosions. For whatever effect he wanted, Jack has often needed to invent a new language while simultaneously saying something in that language, much as Newton had to invent differential calculus in the act of describing the new science of gravity, or Picasso and Braque had to work out the language of Cubism while they were painting in that language. This is a very different kind of creativity – creativity squared, as it were.

His extraordinary restless intelligence underlies the intriguing contradictions in his personality and, thus, in his work. In a typical conversation, Jack wondered why viewers respond as they do to any art, speculating that perhaps we have patterns in our brains and unconsciously try to match a piece of art to those patterns. Kant's *a priori* categories? Or Plato's forms? For someone who doesn't want to intellectualize art, he can be pretty cerebral.

But he is nothing if not contradictory. Jack: the artist using engineering techniques to create disorder and inorganic materials to build organic forms. Jack: the arch-romantic who builds machines, the architect who designs invisible spaces, the magician who conjures with physical laws, the gambler who tries to palm the laws of chance. Above all, Jack is the rational and deliberate artist who is also the irrational and passionate scientist.

Under the guise of simplicity always lie hidden layers of meaning in both this man and his work. Because so much of his art happens in the controlled and highly charged space around it, it seems simple, almost minimalistic. But Jack is simple like a Bach fugue is simple. Imagine for a moment seeing the invisible architectures these pieces generate, the actual light-and sound-spaces they generate, invisible and inaudible to us. It would make the exhibit impossible to navigate. Too many overlapping sensitivities. Too much stimulation. Too much information, and most of it cosmic.

Apart from his disguised complexity, Jack says that most art critics consider him a formalist. "My work is a mixture of subject matter (what we can define) and content (what the viewer feels)." But he is most interested in form, insisting, "An artist is a mechanic of form." Being a formalist for Jack means using engineering principles like Alexander Calder, musical principles like John Cage, space-time principles like the poet T. S. Eliot.

More than for most artists, Jack's work embodies his life – constantly changing relations with invisible radiant energy, creating new patterns within old ones, literally at home in the world and vitally aware of it. Jack's work is about "nature" on every level, from light reflected off ponds to radiation left over from the Big Bang. Fortunately, he shares the world's complex magic with us, and continually makes it beautiful.

"Persistence of vision" aptly describes Jack Dollhausen's thirty-year journey. In our eyes and in our lives, he connects dot to dot, moment to moment, insisting that the dots connect, that we connect with the very large world sparkling, unseen, around us. Jack's pieces forge paths between points through unknown territories, only in tiny lights and mysterious sounds, always flitting ahead of you. Fireflies? Or aliens? You can't catch them, but you can intercept and communicate with them by an intuitive move, for some of us in another dimension. Jack's art is like Shakespeare's island in *The Tempest*; like Prospero, the magician-artist, he tries to transform us earthbound Calibans into fiery Ariels.

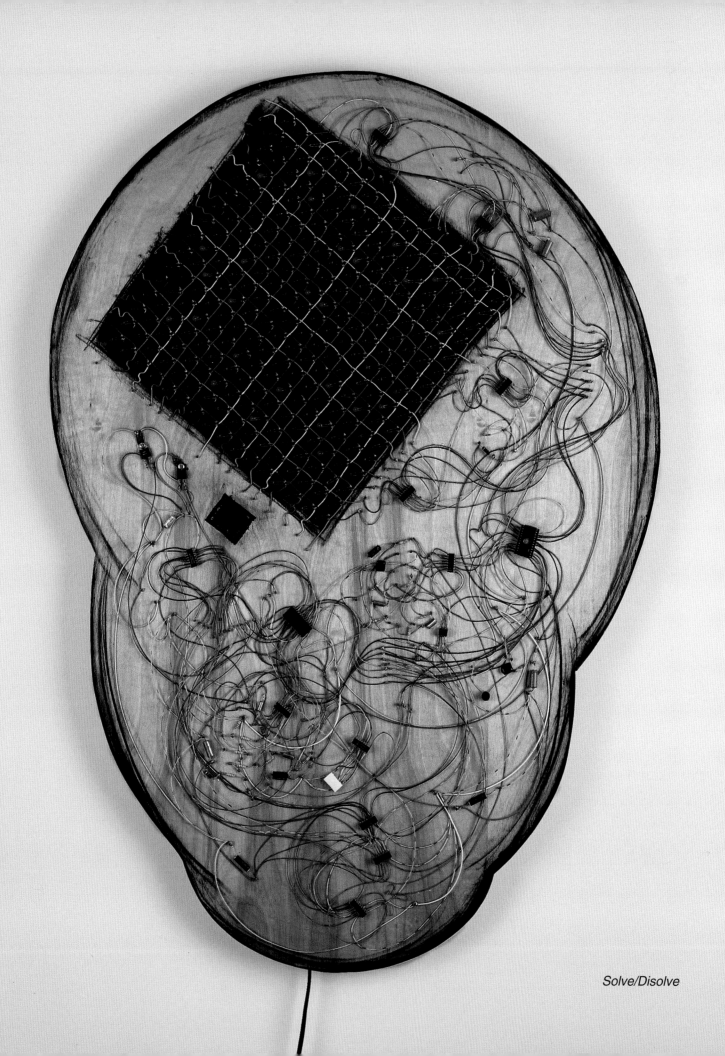

Solve/Disolve

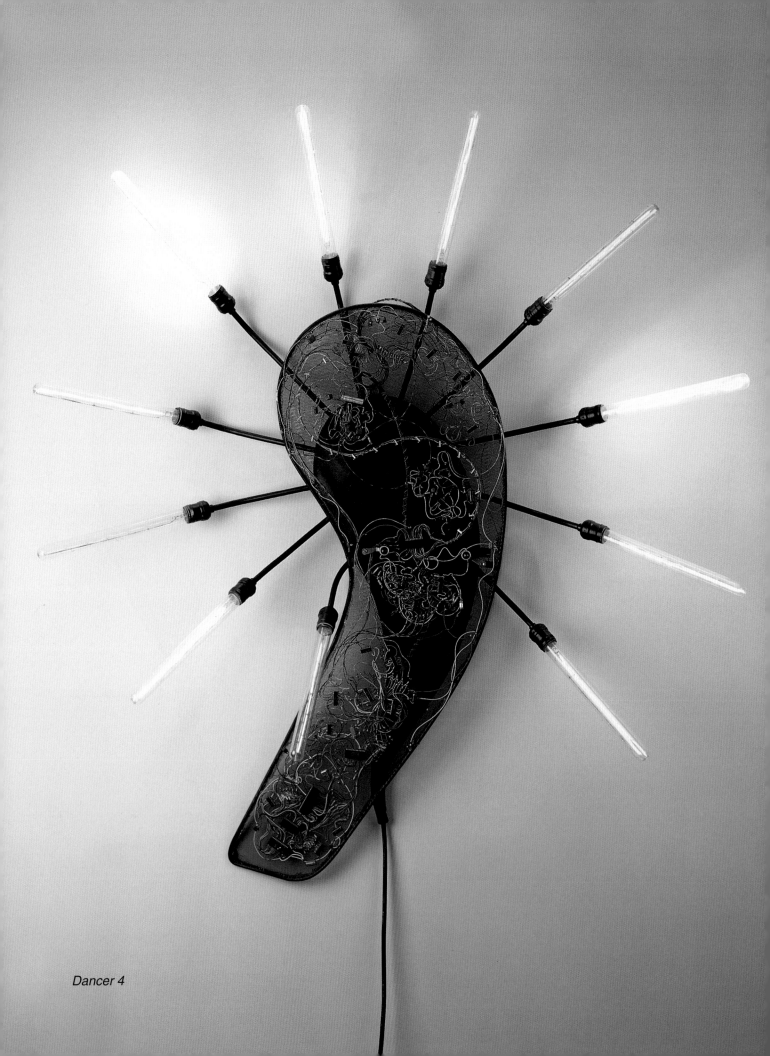

Dancer 4

Constellations of thoughts or feelings. What our

brain synapses would look like in hard wires and

flickering lights. Or what the heart's messages

would look like to different parts of ourselves.

Jack's lights ultimately seem to fire from inner

space, with joy and randomness, spangled as a

good idea. Or love. Conversations with this art

finally become conversations with oneself, which

may be what all good art causes. By bringing

space itself to life, Jack Dollhausen brings us all

to life in a new way as well.

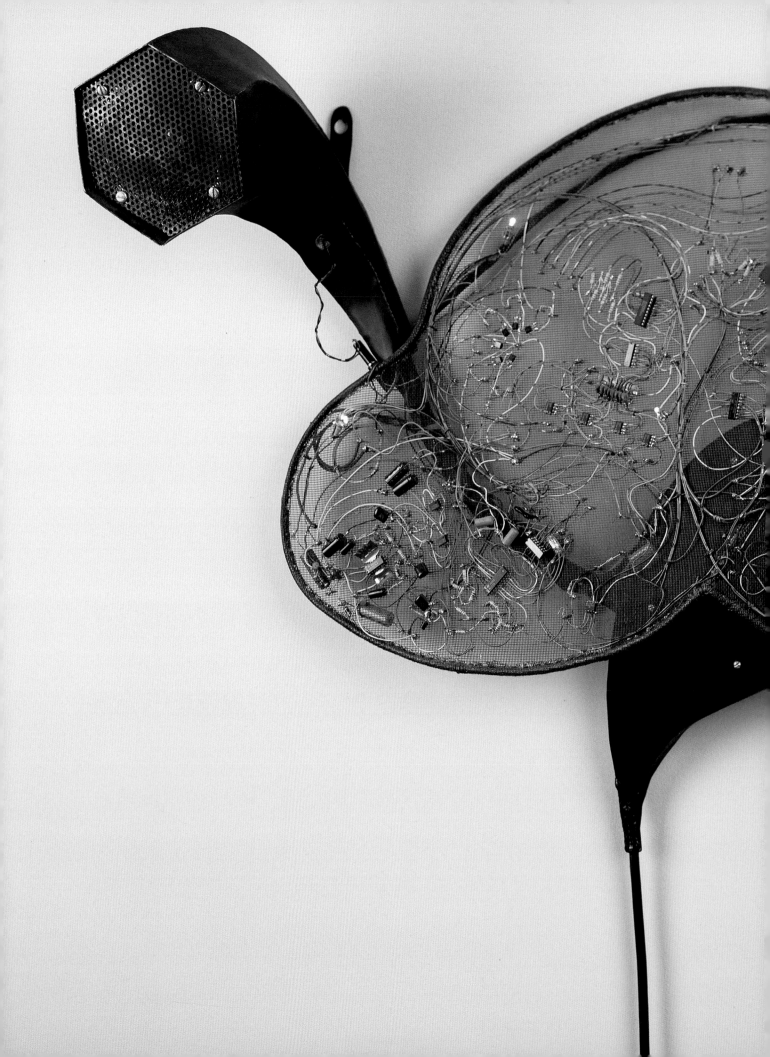

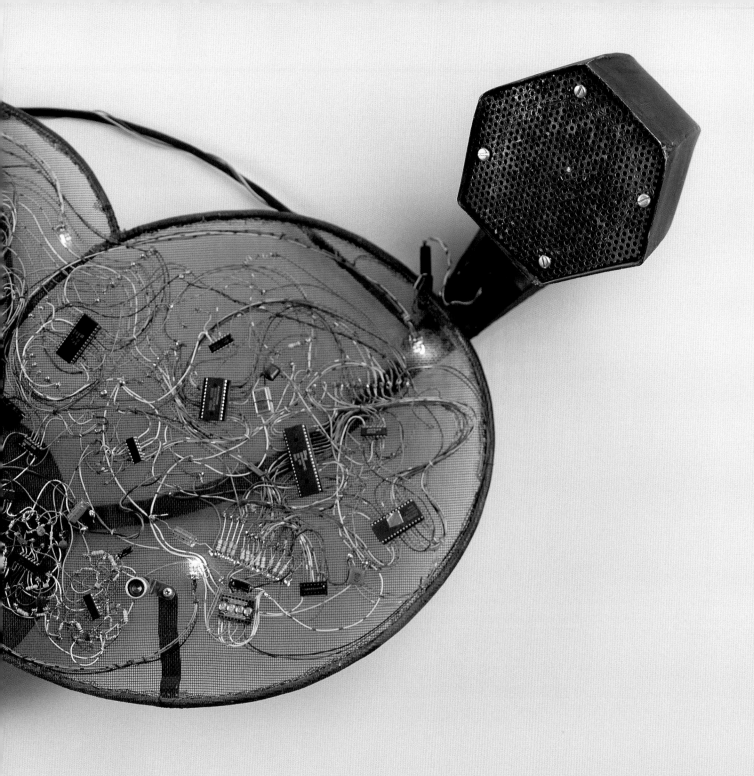

Grace

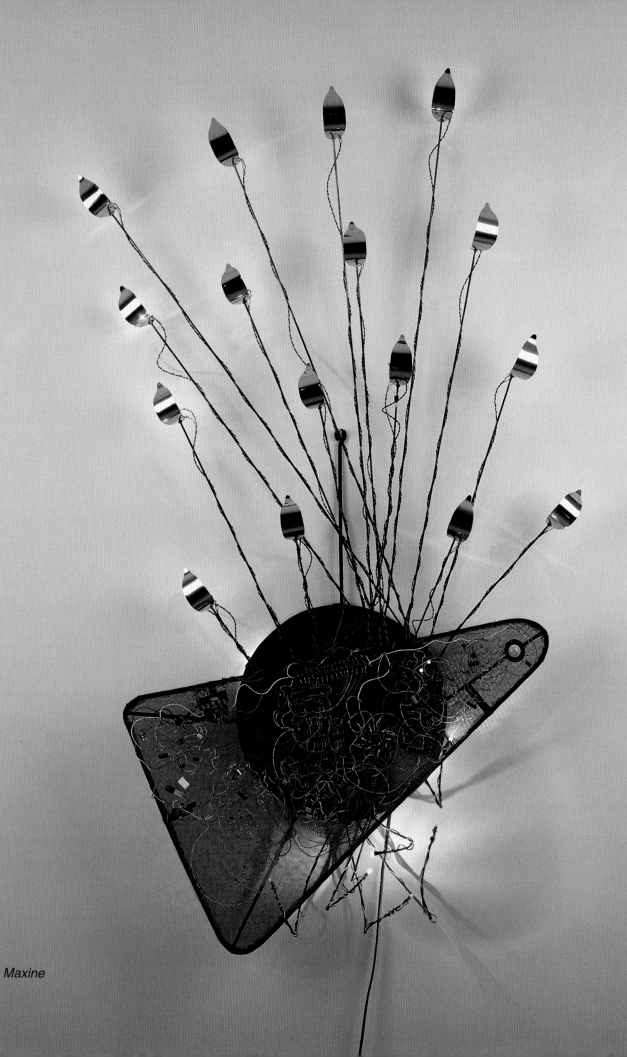

Maxine

JACK DOLLHAUSEN

BORN: 1941
RESIDES: Pullman, Washington

ACADEMIC TRAINING AND DEGREES

1968   M.F.A., Sculpture, Ceramics, Washington State University, Pullman, WA
1966   B.A., Fine Arts, Mathematics, Wisconsin State University, Whitewater, WI
1959 - 63   Civil Engineering, Fine Arts, University of Wisconsin, Madison, WI

OTHER CREDENTIALS

        FCC, First-Class Radio-telephone Operator's License, 1969
        Local 76, Steelworkers (journeyman sheet-metal mechanic)
        Local 166, American Federation of Musicians

PROFESSIONAL ACTIVITIES

1972 -   Professor of Art, Washington State University, Pullman, WA

WASHINGTON STATE ARTS COMMISSION

1993   State Advisory Panel, Art in Public Places, Department of Corrections
1989 - 90   Commissioned Artwork, Spokane Falls Community College, Spokane, WA
1987   Juror, Artist in Schools Program
1985   Juror, Artist Resource Bank

LECTURES, PANELS, SYMPOSIA

2000   Juror, *Northwest Visions* call for artists, Seattle Arts Commission, Seattle, WA
        Juror, Artist Trust GAP grants, Seattle, WA
1998   Juror, *42nd Annual Central Washington Artists Exhibition*, Larson Gallery, Yakima, WA
1996   Lecture, Pan American University, McAllen, TX
        Lecture, McAllen International Museum, McAllen, TX
1995   Lecture, Hoffman Gallery, Oregon School of Arts and Crafts, Portland, OR
1994   Visiting Artist Lecture, University of Wisconsin, LaCrosse, WI
1992   Panelist, *CROSSING POINTS*, A symposium on art and technology, Corvallis, OR
        Visiting Artist, Convocation Address and Public Lecture, Drury College, Springfield, MO
1991   Lecture, Central Washington State University, Ellensburg, WA
        Lecture, Spokane Falls Community College, Spokane, WA
        Lecture, Cheney Cowles Memorial Museum, Spokane, WA
        Lecture, *ART A LA CARTE*, Washington State University, Pullman, WA
        Symposium panel member, *Society-Technology Interface*, Washington State University, Pullman, WA
1987   Visiting Artist, Weber State College, Ogden, UT
1986   Lecture, Cheney Cowles Memorial Museum, Spokane, WA
        Lecture, Art Museum of South Texas, Corpus Christi, TX

SOLO EXHIBITIONS

1998   George Suyama Space, Seattle, WA
1996   McAllen International Museum, McAllen, TX
1995   Hoffman Gallery, Oregon School of Arts and Crafts, Portland, OR
1993   Redmann Galerie, Berlin, Germany
1991   Linda Hodges Gallery, Seattle, WA
        Spokane Falls Community College Gallery, Spokane, WA
1990   Yellowstone Art Center, Billings, MT
1988   Gallery Proper, New York, NY
1987   Redmann Galerie, Berlin, West Germany
1985   Art Museum of South Texas, Corpus Christi, TX

1985	Art Attack Gallery, Boise, ID
	Cheney Cowles Memorial Museum, Spokane, WA
1984	Redmann Galerie, Berlin, West Germany
1981	Montana State University, Bozeman, MT
1980	Boulder Center for the Visual Arts, Boulder, CO
1978	Boise Gallery of Art, Boise, ID
1977	Western Gallery, Western Washington University, Bellingham, WA
	Diablo Valley College, Pleasant Hills, CA
	Eastern Washington Gallery of Art, Cheney, WA
1968	General Electric Light Institute, Cleveland, OH

SELECTED GROUP EXHIBITIONS

2000	*Art & Technology - A Marriage for a New Millennium*, Salem Art Association, Salem, OR
1999	*Action/Reaction - Kinetic Works by Five Sculptors*, McAllen International Museum, McAllen, TX
1998	*Idiomechanisms: A Show of Interactive Sculpture*, Bush Barn Art Center, A. N. Bush Gallery, Salem, OR
1997	*A Distinct Vernacular: Artists of Eastern Washington*, Washington State Convention and Trade Center, Seattle, WA
1995	*Interior Idioms: The Idiosyncratic Art of Eastern Washington*, SeaFirst Gallery, Seattle, WA
1992	*A Celebration of Diversity*, Drury College, Springfield, MO
	P.U.L.S.E., Wichita State University, Wichita, KS
1991	*Faculty + Faculty*, University of Puget Sound, Tacoma, WA
	Artist Made Machines, Corvallis Arts Center, Corvallis, OR
	Northern Lights, Port Angeles Art Center, Port Angeles, WA
	Spirit of the West, West One Travelling Exhibition, ID, OR, WA
1990	*PULSE-2* University Art Museum, University of California, Santa Barbara, CA
	Sound Vision, Center On Contemporary Arts, Seattle, WA
1988-90	*New Perspectives*, Tacoma Art Museum, Tacoma, WA
1987	*The Inland Empire*, Braunstein/Quay Gallery, San Francisco, CA
1985	*Masters of the Inland Northwest*, Cheney Cowles Memorial Museum, Spokane, WA
	Licht, Malerei und Skulptur, Museum of Science, Berlin, West Germany
1984	*Basel International Art Fair*, Basel, Switzerland
	Art Cologne, Cologne, West Germany,
1980	*New Dimensions*, Visual Art Center, Anchorage, AK
1975	*Sculpture Directions*, University of Wisconsin, LaCrosse, WI
	Missoula Museum of the Arts, Missoula, MT
1974	*Art Artists Collect*, California State University, Hayward, CA
1971	*Spokane Annual*, Cheney Cowles Memorial Museum, Spokane, WA

REVIEWS AND ARTICLES

1998	Farr, Sheila. "They Long to be Close to You." *Seattle Times*, November 26.
	Hackett, Regina. "Dollhausen's New Circuits Make Great Connections." *Seattle Post-Intelligencer*, December 4.
1996	"Poesia de la luz y el sonido, a través de sutiles medios electrónicos." *Valle de Texas*, March 20.
1995	"Jack Dollhausen at Hoffman Gallery, Oregon School of Arts and Crafts." *Artweek*, August.
1994	"Charment wie ein Dampf-Radio." *Der Tagesspiegel*, January 3.
1991	"Engaging Artwork." *Spokesman Review*, Spokane, January 18.
	"Interactive Art." *Universe*, Washington State University Press.
	"Jack Dollhausen." *Sculpture*, May/June.
	Kangas, Mathew. "Dossier Northwest." *Sculpture*, May/June.
	Werner Schuman Productions, Smithsonian World, PBS presentation, April 17.
1990	Plous, Phyllis. "Report on a Phenomenon." *Pulse-2*, University of Washington Press, Pullman, WA.
1987	"Jack Dollhausen." Redmann Galerie, Berlin, West Germany.
	Wuff, Jane Elder. "Palettes of the Palouse." *Washington*, V4, #1.
	"10 Jahre Galerie Redmann." Redmann Galerie, Berlin, West Germany.
1985	Platt, Susan. "The Responsive Machine." *Artweek*, March 9.
	Jansen, Johan and Luhrs, Otto. "Licht in Kunst." Museum fur Verkehr und Technik, Berlin, West Germany.

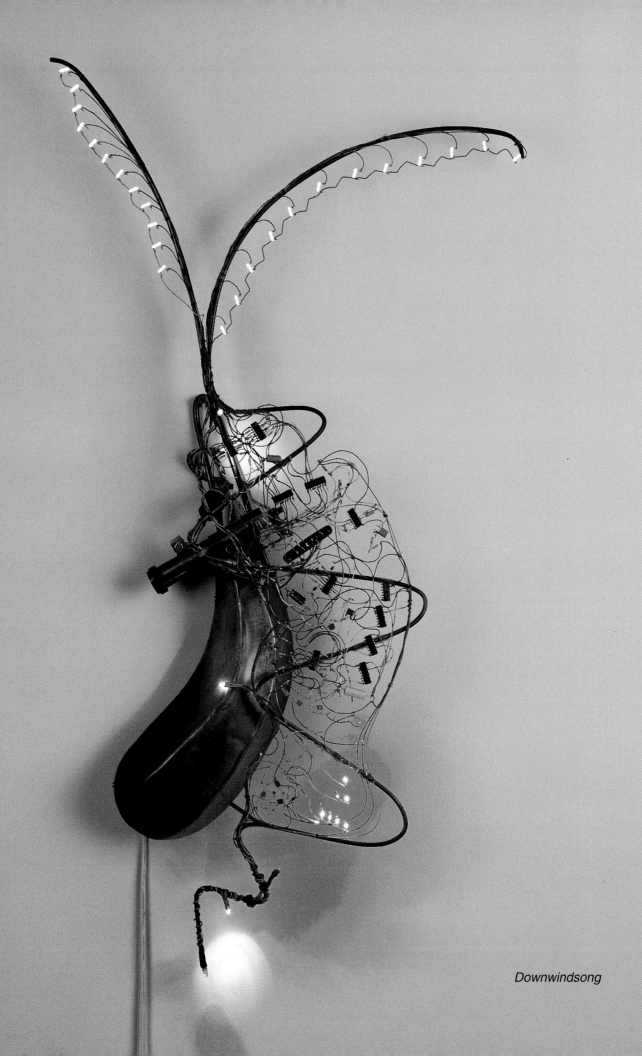

Downwindsong

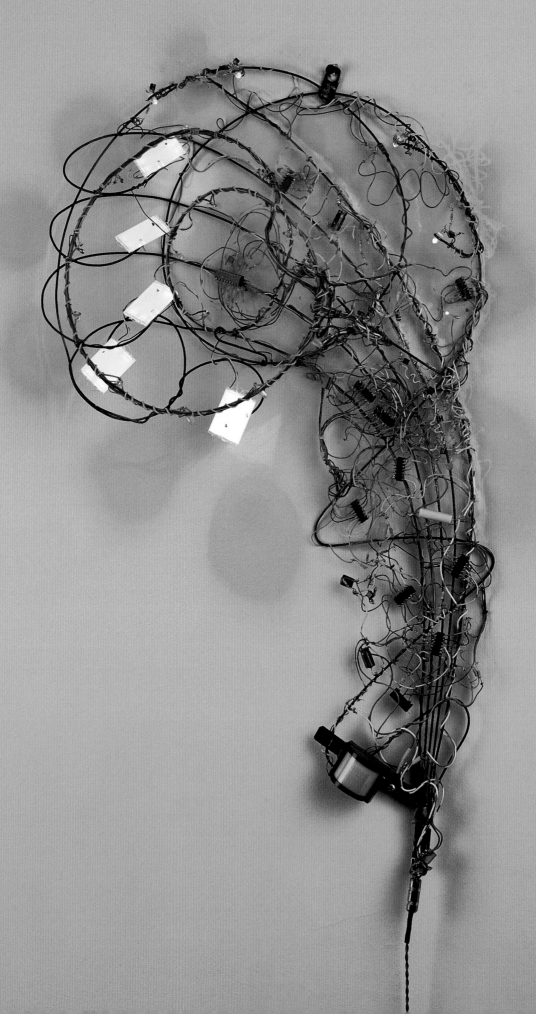

August

1.
Prototype, 1968, wood, electronic circuitry,
27.5 x 14.5 x 4.5", Courtesy of the artist

2.
SPNX, 1972, wood, electronic circuitry,
23 x 28 x 6", Courtesy of the artist

3.
Lightening, 1973 , wood, electronic circuitry,
18 x 15.5 x 3", Collection of David S. and
Deborah Lewy

4.
Piece of Ground, 1975, electronic circuitry,
27 x 19.5 x 2", Courtesy of the artist

5.
Transient Perpetuity, 1976, electronic circuitry,
50 x 15 x 5", Courtesy of the artist

6.
Dancer, 1976, wood, electronic circuitry,
29.5 x 46.5 x 6.5", Collection of Jack Dollhausen,
Courtesy of Beth Sellars

7.
Esu, 1976, wood, electronic circuitry,
24 x 12.5 x 2.5", Courtesy of the artist

8.
Minor Nation (Frog Pond), 1977, wood,
electronic circuitry, 25.5 x 24.5 x 3", Collection
of Boise Art Museum, Boise, ID

9.
Midwest Summer Night's Dream (Bug Jar),
1977, electronic circuitry, 12 x 12 x 8",
Courtesy of the artist

10.
Chance of Laws, 1977, wood, plastic,
electronic circuitry, 34 x 25 x 2.5",
Collection of Ric Collier

11.
A Walk Around the Pond, 1982, wood, electronic
circuitry, 34 x 17 x 5", Courtesy of the artist

12.
Lovesong, 1983, wood, electronic circuitry,
37 x 21 x 3.5", Collection of Northwest Museum
of Arts & Culture, Spokane, WA

13.
Tapestry, 1984, wood, electronic circuitry,
43 x 35 x 7", Collection of Helga Redmann,
Courtesy of the artist

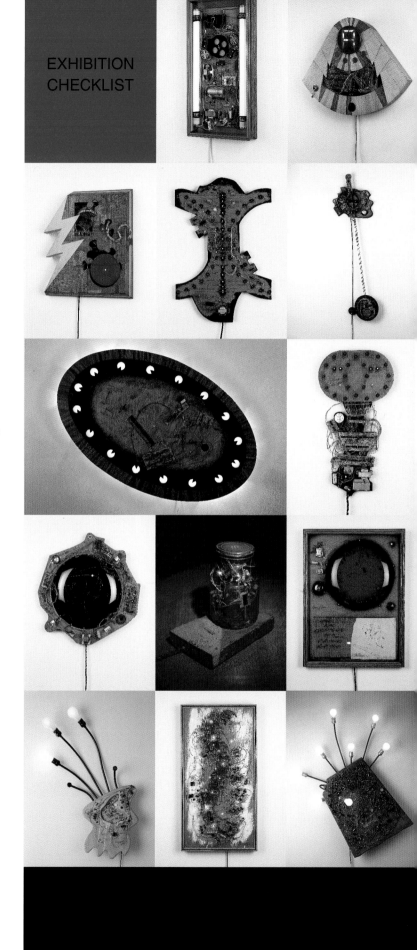

EXHIBITION
CHECKLIST

JACK DOLLHAUSEN A 30 YEAR START

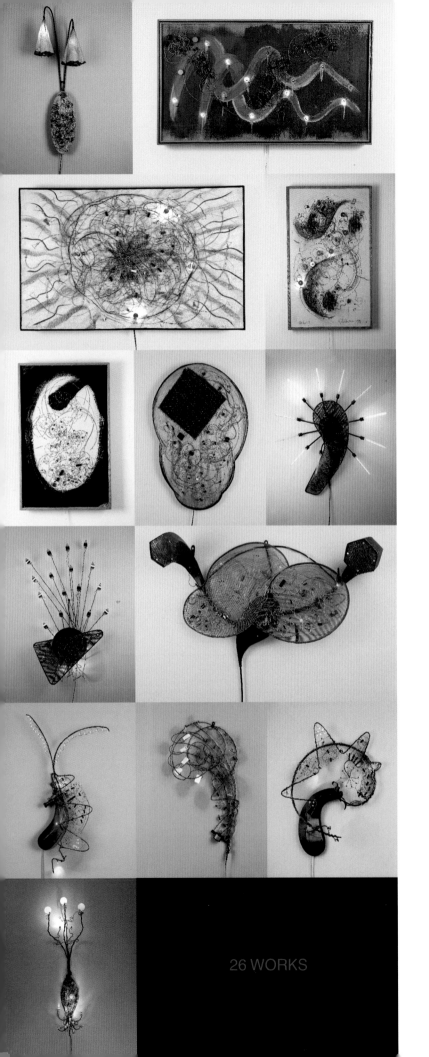

14.
Pinup, 1984, wood, steel, electronic circuitry, 51 x 19 x 13", Collection of Kenneth and Dorothy Holmes, Jr.

15.
Waves, 1984, wood, electronic circuitry, 24 x 43 x 3.5", Collection of Mr. and Mrs. Robert M. Sarkis

16.
Sunflower, 1987, wood, electronic circuitry, 22 x 34 x 3.5", Collection of Helga Redmann, Courtesy of the artist

17.
Too Close, 1988, wood, electronic circuitry, 48 x 31 x 3.5", Courtesy of the artist

18.
Hummin' Stars, 1989, wood, electronic circuitry, 49 x 31 x 4", Courtesy of the artist

19.
Solve/Disolve, 1990, wood, electronic circuitry, 36.5 x 25.5 x 2", Courtesy of the artist

20.
Dancer 4, 1995, electronic circuitry, 54 x 50 x 12.5", Courtesy of the artist

21.
Maxine, 1995, electronic circuitry, 59 x 38 x 8", Collection of Office of the President, Washington State University, Pullman, WA

22.
Grace, 1996, electronic circuitry, 25 x 45 x 11", Courtesy of the artist

23.
Downwindsong, 1998, steel, electronic circuitry, Geiger counter, 34 x 19 x 4.5", Courtesy of the artist

24.
August, 1998, electronic circuitry, 27 x 14.5 x 5.5", Courtesy of the artist

25.
Downwindblue, 1998, cast metal, electronic circuitry, 26 x 22 x 7", Courtesy of the artist

26.
3PPB, 2000, steel, baling wire, infrared sensor, programmable circuit, 28 x 9 x 4.5", Courtesy of the artist

26 WORKS

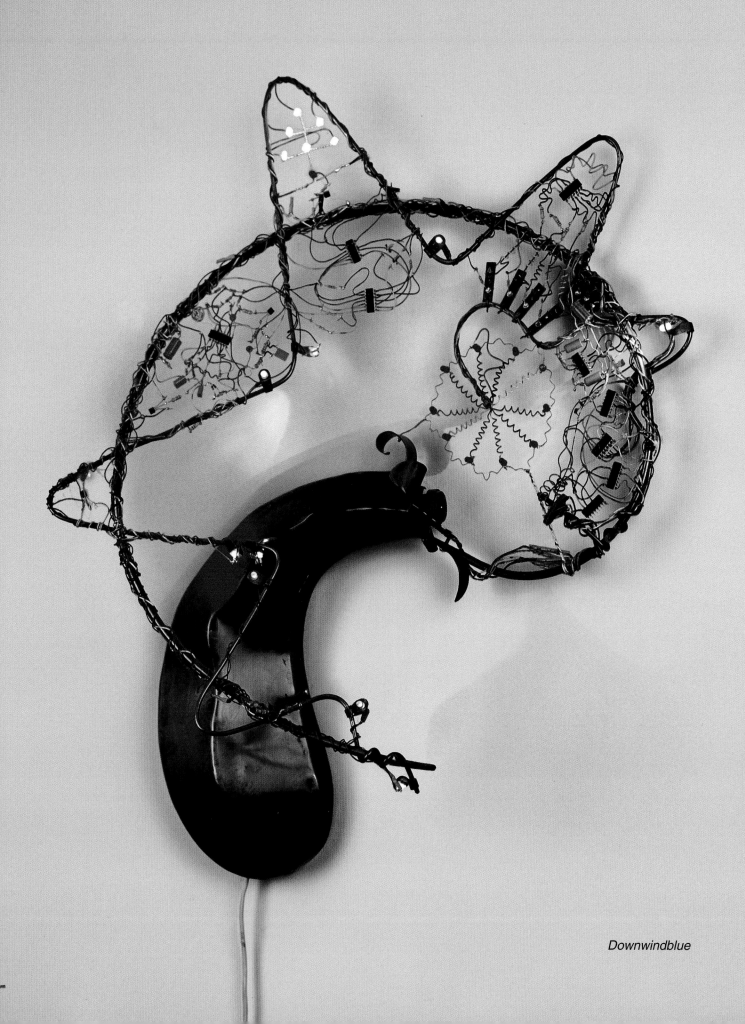

Downwindblue

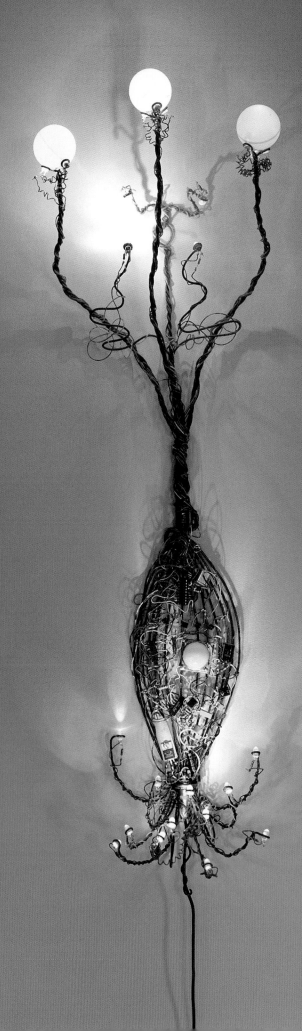